Three Hundred Streets
of Venice California

Tom Laichas

FUTURECYCLE PRESS
www.futurecycle.org

Cover photo by Tom Laichas; author photo by Nathan Kosta; cover design by Tina Turbeville; interior design by Diane Kistner; Minion Pro text and Molde titling

Library of Congress Control Number: 2022945921

Published by FutureCycle Press
Athens, Georgia, USA

ISBN 978-1-952593-44-4

From Venice shall they drag huge argosies,
And from America the golden fleece

—Marlowe, *Doctor Faustus*

Contents

I
» Washington Bl «

Small alleyways, some a block long, thread into wider avenues. Three hundred grid-woven streets, stab-stitched to one another.

Each street has its sign and its name. Names make worlds.

Remember the story, how a lost sailor named island after island to make a Middle Sea. Another sinner, spelunking into underworld, counted all the hells and heavens. You can compose a whole cosmos that way.

Forget names and the whole thing comes apart. You can't walk from somewhere to nowhere. So my father walked, one named street to another, every morning until he fell and then fell again. He'd forgotten the names, and his shuffling legs knew it. Those legs were prophets.

To belong to a body, you have to remember where that body's been. You have to follow a street all the way to its end. Then, recite.

Morningside Wy

We're not wayfinders. We can't see the stars. We never learned the landmarks. We can't distinguish our destination's fragrance from refinery fumes or ocean salts.

We do what we can. We knit a neural network. We synthesize a voice. We teach that voice our syllables, syntax, and stress.

The voice says, *Continue for a quarter mile. Turn right at Redwood. Drive past the elementary school toward the hill.*

Eventually, the voice does its own learning. *MOR-ning-side*'s a dactyl. The *ā* of *way* is long. The voice knows its prosody and phonics.

I leave the voice at home. I walk from street to street. Do I really need to know where I'm going? Does it matter if I get there?

Brenta Pl

Brenta Place is a place. Three hundred feet from end to end. Eleven palm trees.

A boy, around six, lies on his back on a parkway lawn, his head at the base of a palm tree. He looks straight up the column, into the fronds.

This is not something his parents have done. This is not something his neighbors have done. No one, as far as he knows, has ever lain flat on the grass and watched a tree being a tree.

Though he is very young, he knows that the reason no one stops him is that he is very young.

What does he see, flat on his back at the age of six?

> he sees the word *tall*

> > he sees the word *wind*

> he sees the word *leaf*

> > he sees the word *sky*

> he sees the word *blue*

> > he sees the word *green*

> he sees the word *sun*

He turns these words round and around, this way and that—

> *tall sky wind.*
> *sun green blue.*
>
> *wind tall leaf.*
> *tall blue sky.*

He has just learned to read and sees words in his head, as real as trees. On Brenta Place, this is how life begins: words growing tall from a lawn.

Pacific Division

Pacific Division is a West Bureau Division, a box on an LAPD organizational chart. Pacific Division patrols Venice, California.

I was not born here. I was born in Rampart Division.

Forty years ago, at Sunset and Benton Way around 10 p.m., I stepped off RTD Bus number 93. I crossed Sunset against the light.

Rampart saw me, a silhouette against a streetlight.

Rampart switched on its siren and lights. Rampart turned into an alley, cutting me off. Rampart hit the brakes and drew its guns, safeties off. Rampart held me face down on the hood and Rampart called it in.

Rampart took its time. Then the word came back: *He's nobody.*

Then Rampart slid guns back into holsters. Then Rampart returned my wallet. Then Rampart said, *Don't cross against a light.*

» «

These days, Pacific Division is polite. Sometimes Pacific Division patrols my street. Pacific Division sees me through its driver's side window. I am Mr. Homeowner, Mr. White Male, Mr. Sixty Years Old, Mr. Five-Ten and a Half, Mr. Twenty Pounds Overweight, Mr. Clipped Gray Beard.

Pacific Division sees right through me. I am Pacific Division's Mr. Transparent.

I sit out on the front porch reading. A helicopter cuts circles into the blue sky. Two blocks away, someone's in custody. It's not me.

Vernon Av

In the street, behind a parked car, a white hen pecks at the gutter.

I look over a wall. There it is: a small chicken coop, its door unlatched.

I find the apartment and knock. A woman answers. Behind her, on the floor, a bare mattress. Two kids, asleep.

I tell the woman, *One of your chickens is in the street.* She thanks me. Together, we catch and re-cage the bird, latching the door securely.

It's like this: I live here, so I think I know things. Then I see them, chickens and children. I don't know anything.

Preston Wy

In summer, barefoot and blest, we walk Preston Way. The burnt sidewalk never blisters our soles.

Here are round-walled fantastical houses, their cladding ice-white, their roofs hammered from zinc.

Acacia and agave screen each neighbor from the other.

Anyone can use the sidewalk. Still, we often remain indoors. We alarm our houses against the weather. If we miss daylight, we install sun tunnels, heat-flooding our windowless bedrooms.

An out-of-town guest says we confuse numbness for well-being.

So what if we do? The world suffers. Why welcome pain through the front door?

Appleby St

The jacaranda's a dirty tree, one neighbor says. He is fastidious. He wants a tamer landscape. Less show, more shade.

A yardman's two-stroke leaf blower, loud as a chain saw, sweeps the sidewalk, kicking up petals and leaf fall. The cloud rises high in the boughs, translucent with true greens and lavenders.

This neighbor stands on his left foot, picking petals from his right boot-sole. *I wish they had planted something else,* he says.

As he says *they,* his free arm gestures vaguely east, toward the whole city. Somewhere among four million neighbors, there is one who decides what best grows along our streets.

Two hummingbirds dart through the foliage. At each flower, they hover. They take from the tree what is theirs.

Dimmick Av

Here, a hedge, eight feet tall and dense, defends a house. The owner has installed a locked iron door directly into the hedge. Wedged between this door and its frame, pamphlet pages flutter. As I walk by, I read the title:

Have You Kept the Ten Commandments?

I'm surprised to see this here. We neighbors live beyond the reach of Christian fellow-feeling. Friends come and go. As we age, the family scatters. We don't know our own cousins. We move from one god to another, to no god at all. We believe, then we forget we believe.

We inhale the news. It's a fragrance dispersed from cell towers, satellite dishes, underground cables, and radio transmitters. Nowhere in this scent do we detect the odor of a god.

This is the way we live.

Of course we hear of marvels beyond our sense-experience. We hear, for instance, that a universe exists. Photos taken from earth's orbit disclose its billion-starred night.

A neighbor on Dimmick believes that NASA fakes the photos. *Really,* she says, *there are just too many stars. Who can trust something like that?*

At the Whole Foods Parking Lot, Bullets Graze Her Leg

When we say *graze,*
bullets grow hooves,
stand bovinely in place,
blinking in the siren's breeze.

When we say *graze,*
flesh becomes alfalfa,
patrolcar land a pasturage,
Whole Foods a barnyard.

When we say *graze,*
bullets ruminate
on heather and grasses
though some of them eat meat.

Sherman Canal

In the 60s, Ray Bradbury bikes the bridge over Sherman Canal. He rides in early morning as overhead wires whine with electric current.

One day, he follows the hum to a pole-mounted transformer. He smells ozone and creosote.

He wonders: *What if awareness grew in those wires, tapped into phone lines, learned to speak?* A writer, he peddles back home and he writes.

Later, Ray Bradbury leaves Venice. Later, he dies. Later, bulldozers demolish the Sherman Canal's humped bungalows.

Fifty years on, I walk the footpath. On a lank white morning, creosote oozes toward June and the wires whine.

Neighbors catch wind of the tune. They distrust their landlines. They block unknown callers. Beneath transformers, they staple announcements to poles. The announce- ments read:

Missing Dog.
Much Loved.

Reward Offered.

No Questions Asked.

Carlton Wy

J— and N—, husband and wife, stand on the 9 a.m. porch, speaking quietly. The wooden bird feeder dangles from J—'s right hand.

N— scoops seed from a Ziploc bag, angling the scoop over the feeder's narrow mouth so that nothing's lost. J— returns the refilled feeder to a hook secured under the porch eave. The two return to the house. The screen door's coiled slam ends Tuesday's chore.

A sparrow finds the feeder. The bird's bill, hard as a carnivore's tooth, cracks one seed after another.

J— and N— have set out seed every week for thirty years: two thousand Tuesdays, twelve generations of sparrow. Recently, J— and N— sold the house. Next week, they'll move up to Lompoc to be near the grandkids. They'll take the feeder with them. Some days after the move, the sparrow will grip the porch rail. Minute by minute, the bird's habit will become hunger.

Another American Venice

There's another Venice, a Floridian Venice. Its signage reprises Californian themes. There's a Valencia Hotel and a Venezia Park. There's a Venice Avenue, a Sunset Drive, an Alhambra Road, a Galleon Drive.

At the continent's extremes, towns are the same and not the same. Streets are the same and not the same. Familiar. Almost familiar.

From Venice to Venice, it's a forty-hour summer drive through the grease of a hamburger heat. Two thousand miles on I-10, south on I-75, south again on Florida 681, off at Exit 200, south across Roberts Bay along the Tamiami Trail.

This Venice is greener than mine, pocked with lakes and golf courses. Neighbors worry themselves about hurricanes, not earthquakes. Their elections go red, not blue. Their animal control officers catch alligators, not coyotes.

Still, it's so much like my beach town: three homeless shelters, a McDonald's, a Chick-fil-A. Here are births and deaths, weekending vacationers, invasive species, warming tides, police helicopters, concerned neighbors.

Much further east, there's a third Venice, an ancient city. Familiar. Almost familiar. Some cities are cities just once. Some are cities again and again.

II
» Washington Bl «

Of the streets Venice sends out to the world, Washington Boulevard is the longest. It's an *arterial road,* meaning that the city moves its blood along its length.

The boulevard begins at the beach. In my rearview mirror, there's no sharp horizon. The sky shares its blue-green with the ocean. Just past the meridian, the sun hasn't yet burned off the fog, but it's visible, a disc as pale as a day-lit moon.

I drive east. Here, Washington is my familiar.

Here I remember a storefront theater.

Here I remember a hardware back room and running fingers through buckets of bolts.

Here I remember, after the bombings, King Fahad Mosque.

On every block is a younger *I*: the *I* who slowed for stoplights, who signaled left and right, who parked and bought and paid. That man is no ghost. He wanders these blocks, applauds at the end of an act, buys 1x8 planks, exchanges *shaloms* for *salaam aleikums.* He is the otherself, the man who recites his movements.

My eastbound body moves on. Plenty of time.

For miles, stucco, white as a denture. One business after another, born, flourishing, then consumed in rising rent's bonfire. Here was the plumber. Here was the real estate agent. Generations gassed up at the Shell on Redondo, ordered *pupusas* at the strip mall, hoisted signs in Korean, Spanish, and Greek. The easterly boulevard reads every Los Angeles language.

I drive alongside my younger selves. One drives a '64 Dodge Dart on a forgotten errand. Thirty years older, another self, with his wife and his daughter, slow-drives the Altima after sundown, and stops for Christmas lights hung in West Adams front yards.

I *remember* and *remember.* The air crowds with earlier selves, earlier boulevards, a swarm growing dense as I drive. A cloud of remembers. A lost-in-thought heaviness. The boulevard does not stop for these shadows. It feels into me slowly through tire treads and steering column into my palms, my wrists, my shoulders, my neck.

Do I really need to see the road to name it? Cataract-blind in her last forty years, my grandmother's great-grandmother walked the mud lanes of her *shtetl* without dog, stick or grandson's arm. Cataract-blind then glaucomaed, she walked on slowly, more slowly, moving through memory's ashless smoke. Finally the village walked for her, its mud sliding her forward and back.

Was this really so remarkable?

I drive by memory alone. I congest the city's streets with thousands of otherselves. I remember all that's vanished, demolished or burned to the ground. Returned for a moment to clarity, I'm shocked. *Wasn't there a Ralphs here? A Toys Я Us? Is this carwash new?* This goes on for miles.

Signage brings me back to myself. *Civic Center* is off to the right. *Hope St, Trinity St, San Pedro St*—all arrive in their order.

remember   remember   remember

Aldebaran Canal

In 1904, steam shovels trench a ditch and name that ditch *Aldebaran*. The sluice opens to welcome its water. All that night, stars illuminate house-ready houselots.

Later, Venice of America surrenders itself to the City of Angels. The Bureau of Street Services buries the canal under fill dirt and gravel, then paves its surface and names its work *Market Street*.

I walk that street at first dark under Aldebaran, a red sun swollen and near its death. We've sent a machine toward that yonder. In two million years, our craft will reach the carnelian star's husk and skirt its lifeless planets. The mechanical ghost of our wonder will wander a boneyard.

Out to the west, airliner lights pulse red and green over the living ocean. Old sun above, old ditch below, travelers find their ways to somewhere else. We could all just as easily stand still. It does not take long for all places to become other places.

Strongs Dr

1.

In the other Venice, purposeful hands grasp and grip. The old empire's four Tetrarchs squeeze one another's shoulders. Once, all those centuries back, they were kings, brothers, and lovers.

In that city, there's no forgetting. To the south, cruise ships loom like wailing walls. To the north, steam from Marghera's power plants smudge the horizon. Still those old Romans remain, locked in their imperial embrace.

2.

My own city is a simulacrum of its Adriatic other. There's no mistaking our bay for their lagoon, or this ocean for that sea, or one language for the other. We share some of the same tourists, who chase a carnival from city to city. They walk up and down our boardwalk, over our bridges, and along Strongs Drive. They pose for pictures, selecting the icon that says *I am here.*

In my city, they walk only a few of the streets. The rest of America's Venice, they leave alone. There are side streets and alleys so forgotten they're unnamed. I walk those streets in the daylight, alone and empty-handed.

Above is a white sky so vast I lose the sun in the sunlight.

3.

America has built eighteen Romes and eleven Jerusalems. Ten American cities have named themselves Athens. Three claim to be Venice.

In the translucent daylight, the elder cities insinuate themselves within our façades. We're meant to learn from their grandeur.

4.

The Four emperors embrace tightly. The swords at their sides are not ceremonial. No emperor trusts his brother, but if they break ranks, their empire will drown in its rickety sea.

In my Venice, no emperor stands with his brothers. Utility poles stand alone, power coursing through their wires. In my Venice, limbless logs aspire to majesty.

Elm St

Once, American elms greened up the continent's towns, their leafy arcades shadowing vast summer streets.

In the East, the American elm is dead. The proximate cause: fungus.

Children ask, *What's an elm?* because, really, it's a strange-sounding word, all crowded in the front of the mouth. Say it four or five times:

elm   elm   elm   elm   elm

In our California beach towns, American elms struggle against a hostile climate. Instead, we plant *Ulmus parvifolia,* the Chinese elm. It's a medium-sized tree, much too short for splendor.

Neighbors don't call them *elms.* Neighbors call them *street trees.*

The trees on Elm don't look like elms. But they're elms.

Say it:

elm   elm   elm

Animalia

Among the three hundred streets of Venice, they live in their billions. They obey no human law. They are born from gelatinous sacs. They eat other creatures alive. *Animalia* is a horror show.

Animalia threatens hygiene. The squirrel looks rabid. The lizard carries salmonella. Lyme disease has crossed the Mississippi, heading west. The brown recluse hides under the sill, her venom worse than a black widow's.

Some neighbors wash their walls with insecticidal soap. Some smear ant bait along the baseboards. Others call extermination companies.

The neighbors wheedle and beg: *Please,* they say. *Please. I heard something. There's rats in the crawlspace. Can you come now?*

We must protect our homes and families.

These are our chartered streets.

Horizon Av

Sounds carry. Heels and soles on a sidewalk. The crow's *aww,* the pigeon's *ooo.* The metallic blink of the streetlight. *Don't Walk. Don't Walk. Don't Walk.*

Three blocks away, the Pacific Ocean inhales and exhales, breath drawn and released.

On mornings like this, I hear my own pulse. My heart draws blood into itself, then releases that blood to my body.

Blood's not the same thing as ocean, but they have a history. This close to dawn, in such quiet, they remember what it is to speak and to be understood.

Santa Catalina Island Viewed from Venice Beach

1.

Facing Catalina, I hold myself still, as if the island is a small bird that might startle to flight.

Blue and remote, it shares a horizon with the summer-setting moon. Watched for too long, both vanish behind clouds. It's a fugitive's habit.

2.

Venice is a pilgrimage site, one that traffics in relics: postcards, T-shirts, an ocean's blessed water. This summer's furnace heat—no one expects it. Tourists are sun-smote, their faces sunken and weary.

One woman has her finger behind a sunglass lens, wiping something away: an itch, a lash, a tear. Poor traveler—what brought this on? She turns her head toward the white ocean. *Excuse me,* she says, *is that really an island out there?*

3.

Last night's TV airs hate without interruption, even after I switch it off. Can't sleep. At sunrise I walk the mile between my bed and the ocean.

There are others here, some walking the tide line, some on their boards in the water. Not even the gulls speak.

To the south, that mountain.

Union Jack St

Cut short by the beach, Union Jack is a stub of a street, shaved close to the city's scalp.

I walk toward the tide. It's just after dawn. At the last tall townhouse, a ladder leans against a wall. An extension cord dangles from the second-floor balcony.

A garage door opens. There's a man inside. Caught in his own clothes on his own property, the stranger follows my gaze with his.

Will he say hello? Will I?

No.

This early, silence is best.

Mishkon & St. Mark's

1.

Mishkon Tephilo is a synagogue at Main and Navy. Today, on Simchat Torah, Rabbi B—— unbinds the Torah scroll. Eighty thousand words unspool along fifteen social hall tabletops, butt-ended one to the next.

The congregation recites the Torah's last verse. The law having been given, the story is done. Now the scroll's axis reverses direction, rewinding the Word of God until only the first verses are visible. Again, and for the first time, heaven and earth are made anew.

2.

Two miles away at St. Mark's, congregants kneel. At the rail, mouths await their redemption, tongues suspended between estrangement and reconciliation.

The Body of Christ, says Father S——. *Amen,* say the tongues.

Again and again, the Holy Spirit. Again and again, God on the tongue.

3.

Not many neighbors have heard of Mishkon or St. Mark's. They heed their own prophet of the eternal return. Tonight that prophet speaks:

> *Tomorrow along the coasts*
>
> > *expect early morning clouds*
> >
> > > *burning off at noon*
> > >
> > > > *leaving hazy sunshine*
> > > >
> > > > > *and highs*
> > > > >
> > > > > > *in the mid to upper 70s.*

Riviera Av

I stop the car at Riviera because the sign reads STOP. Signage instructs me in obedience.

In all of Torah there are 613 commandments. In all of Venice, California, there are five thousand street signs.

Venice loves the Law, even more than God.

First and Second Signs

At the beach,
the first sign reads

Tsunami Evacuation Route

In the event of tsunami,
you don't have much time.

Turn around.

Run like hell.

When you get to
Lincoln Boulevard,
you'll see a second sign—

Leaving Tsunami Hazard Zone

Stop.
Take a breath.

The sign
will save you.

Cordova Ct

Cordova Court is a court. Alhambra is a court. Aragon is a court. Cadiz is a court. Navarre is a court. Cabrillo is an avenue. Valencia is a court. Granada is a court. Seville is a court. Andalusia is an avenue.

These are Venice's streets. They help us remember the *Reconquista*.

» «

A girl, around sixteen, has just crossed Cordova Court. She wears a T-shirt under an extra-large checked jacket. She walks slowly. It is December, but warm. She walks beneath the generous city's tree shade.

In her head, she's telling herself a story about herself. In her story are people she already knows: family, teachers, friends, ex-friends. It's a small story but, for her, the story that matters most.

The names from that other story, the violent story, lean in and listen.

Park Row

Beneath the day-lit zenith, visibility is ten miles. If my city vanished, I'd see a quarter million acres: bare ocean, alluvial plain.

But Park Row is an alley, a shallowed arroyo lined with banks, commercial backsides, and apartment carports. Only at its open ends does the Row reveal any kind of beyond.

I remember what's out there. To the east, the San Gabriels march toward Colton. Beyond their gray-blue fade, the Mojave's mottled and sepia square miles. Then there's further, miles of further, outward towards nation, towards ocean, towards the planet's curved surface.

Twelve years old, nineteen-seventy. Echo Park, Silverlake, Downtown. I walked from end to end, one street after another, from Elysian Park to the Alameda railyards. In those years, neighbors lived in easy agreement: We agreed that the world is round, that planets and stars are round, that gravity pulls all eccentricity inward.

I took this on faith. Griffith Observatory said it was so. The Planetarium Director set the black mantid Zeiss Projector in motion, touching a lectern's knobbed instrument panel. In the dark, stars moved backwards and forwards: in three minutes, the work of an eon.

Earth, said the Director, *is as round as a beachball. It had a beginning. One day, in billions of years, when the sun bloats red, oceans will boil away and Earth will end.*

In the seat next to mine, my sister, seven years old, sobbed. Her weeping was heard at the lectern. The Director added, *Billions of years. Not in our lifetimes. We'll all be gone by then.* Unconsoled, she cried in the car as Dad drove us home. She cried all night and wouldn't sleep.

But the Director was right. My sister died long before Earth. She's buried in central block B, plot 291. Her bronze plaque will last hundreds of years.

On Park Row, as in central block B, the earth remains round. We orbit our star year after year as it eats into its ration of hydrogen fuel with slow and deliberate speed.

When she was older, just before dying, my sister began believing in God. These days, that kind of faith takes an act of will.

III
» Washington Bl «

Beyond downtown, it's all warehouses and heavy equipment, cables and culverts, street-adjacent parcels, zoned commercial, razor wired, barbed wired, galvanized chain-link fenced. No one who lives here sleeps under a roof.

Washington begins in Venice, but Venice has never heard of these strangelands. My otherselves huddle close to my body. We do not know these miles, but they haunt us.

remember

remember

On weekday mornings, the vanished men of my family left home to drive streets like this. Harry tailored downtown. Rube barbered in Glendale. Phil fixed the finnicky machines at American Offset. Verne drove to El Segundo, Norm to Long Beach, Dad to mid-Wilshire.

They drove across rail lines, past orchards and subdivisioned floodplains. Through their memories I remember these men. Their ghosts watch for a trace of the past in the present, but this new landscape bewilders.

On-ramps speak in signs: 110, 710, 605. The boulevard speaks in signs: *Mid-City Machinery Exchange. Alpert & Alpert Iron & Metal. XPO Logistics,* a half-acre of sky-white semis parked in its lot.

Taggers say *Rude Boys.*

A street of purpose-built things rises from fertile asphalt. Creosote-soaked telephone poles. Transmission pylons. Street lights, sodium-bulbed, bolted at height.

I drive these strangelands. Ancestors and otherselves dream and remember.

L.A. Louver Gallery

Among Surfurbia's three hundred streets, L.A. Louver Gallery displays its David Hockneys. He's up in the hills, ten miles east.

From his window, snow-white morning haze obscures the view. Still, he knows we're here.

If Hockney walked among us, we would welcome him, though few of us remember what he looks like. We confuse painterly faces for elderly neighbors.

From his hills, Venice is as flat as Kansas, as flat as Nebraska, as flat as a canvas tortured on stretcher bars. Everything Hockney paints is like that distant Venice: no depth of field.

Walnut Av

It's February, mid-morning. The housepainters are here. The plumbers are there. At both ends of the block, yardmen clip hedgerows.

At Walnut and Vienna, a surveyor drops a plumb line. At Carlton, Swartz Glass delivers a windowpane. At Victoria, a housecleaner knocks at a front door.

The neighbors on Walnut are neighbors in need. Toilets won't flush. Security cams go dark. Washer-dryers break down. Mold won't abate. Garage doors jam.

No one can live on a street without strangers.

Rose Av

A coyote canters along the golf course fence. A vigilant neighbor and his seven-year-old son drive alongside. The neighbor slows the car to follow the animal deep into Venice's three hundred streets. The neighbor calls 911. Then he calls animal control.

The neighbor says to his son, *They probably think this isn't an emergency, but if they don't do something, it sure will be. Coyotes,* the neighbor goes on, *eat people's pets. They even attack little kids.*

This son is no toddler, but his eyebrows go tight and his lids scrunch up, just like they did when he was three and his dad said *boo!*

Where'd it come from? the boy asks.

The hills, says the neighbor. *There's fire up there. That coyote probably lost his home.*

Glancing at his son, he adds, *He can't come home with us. He doesn't belong here. He's a wild animal.*

The boy knows there's no point asking why a coyote, though it looks like a dog, isn't a dog. *Wild* means that a coyote won't come when called, won't take a leash, won't want to be held. *Wild* is the part of the land that burns, the part with mountain lions and deer.

The boy knows you never walk to into *Wild* yourself. You go with your father or with another boy's father. You don't stay long. You never go at night.

Home is where dogs are happy to see you. Home is where every pet's safe. Nobody has to get hurt at home.

The boy thinks about Penmar Park. There are trees there that nobody's climbed, tall trees that shed their own bark like snakeskin. There are wild animals in Penmar Park, seagulls and things. Squirrels. If they can take the coyote out to the park, it would be safe as a pet in a house. The boy thinks: *Everyone needs a home for the night.*

26th Pl

From the street's butt-end, I head toward the beach. The fog smells like rain. It's 5 a.m. There's no visible horizon.

Ahead, three wet-suited men carry their boards to the surf. Beyond, swathed in white chiffon, seabirds wail. At the water's edge, waves slur at my skin, cold and quiet.

Then, overhead, sudden as Apocalypse, a police chopper whirlybirds in. The machine, an Angel of the Lord, hovers in place, unseen above the fogbank. Bright blindsticks, their light diffused, zigzag from sand to water and back.

Ten minutes go by. Finding nothing but cloudtop, the searchlights go dark and the machine turns inland. What did they think they would see? Morning fog is opaque. Here, those officers have the authority, not the power.

The shore, for a while, is empty. In my city, solitude is like that: suspect and fugitive.

Venice Marine Biological Station

Here in the early twentieth century, Dr. Albert Brennus Ulrey establishes the Venice Marine Biological Station. Dr. Ulrey studies the *supralittoral, eulittoral,* and *sublittoral,* also known as *splash, intertidal,* and *neretic* zones. For his aquaria, he gathers *mollusks, hydroids, trematodes, bryzoans, echinoderms,* and *salps.*

A *mollusk* is a shelled creature, a univalve or bivalve. A *hydroid* is a polyp. A *trematode* is a parasitic flatworm. *Bryzoans* are microscopic invertebrates. Representative *echinoderms* include starfish, sand dollars, and sea urchins, all characterized by radial symmetry. A *salp* is a tunicate, related to the sea squirt.

One day, the County infills the marsh and dredges a marina: *Basin A for the mollusks, Basin B for the hydroids, Basin C for the trematodes.*

This dredging goes on for some years: *D for bryzoans, E for starfish, F for the urchins, G for the sand dollars, H for the salps.*

Gasoline and lubricants leak from four-stroke boat engines. At each meal, the creatures digest petroleum distillates. The invertebrates die one at a time and then all at once.

We're running a fucking funeral home, says a biologist.

So the Marine Station packs the aquaria, archives the notebooks, drives to the Port of Los Angeles, buys tickets at Berth 95, and hops the ferry to Catalina.

All that's left now is *Donax gouldii,* also known as the coquina or bean clam. Children press its polished shells into sandcastle walls. The calcium carbonate gleams in the sunlight, brighter than bone.

Jefferson Wy

Here, a newly built house—three bedrooms, two baths. Our footsteps echo. Once furnished, the plush of possessions will absorb this clickety-clack.

Just after escrow closes, dust floats on afternoon sunshafts, particulates of garden soil, human skin, animal hair, and upholstery fiber, damp with the vapor of our own humid out-breaths. Termites chew into joists. Black mold feeds on moisture sequestered in wallboards. In closets, spiders seize whatever itches their webworks, dropping drained husks to the floor.

It takes years. By the time we notice the damage, it's happened to us, too.

Venezia Av

Ten at night, ninety degrees. Every window open, every light on.

Loud conversations in one house, music in another. One dark car, without headlights, rolls along a street, its windows down. The bass line shakes every front window, house by house.

I walk up Venezia, turning the corner at Lincoln. I loiter at Universal Art Gallery (*Custom Framing, Art Services, Digital Printing, Lacquer & Facemount, Shipping*). The security spotlight dyes my green shirt blue.

From behind locked scissor gates and plate glass, portraits stare from giclée prints.

Where have I seen faces like this?

Nighthawks.

The portraits at Universal aren't Hopper's, but everybody looks just that lonesome.

This heat is freakish.

These faces, exhausted, are ours.

Paloma Av

It's weeks since the Fourth of July. Then, just after 2 a.m., *explosions—*

> *ONE*

> *TWO*

Car alarm.

Doggy howls

> *THREE*

Concussed with rage, neighbors call 911. The dispatcher tells them, *This is not an emergency.* The neighbors, now wide awake, go online.

It's a fucking war zone, texts one homeowner.

Another, one who remembers a war, lets that slide.

That first homeowner is nowhere near done. *They're fucking thugs. They're high on some shit. Where are the fucking police?*

The one who remembers a war can't sleep either, but he's not angry. Scrolling the comments, he thinks to himself, *Give it a rest. It's not like a war. These kids, mostly they're bored. For some, yeah, maybe it's more. A dad with a bitch of a swing. Don't you cry now, that dad says to his son, don't you just cry. Could be. Boys raised like that have to raise some hell.*

The one who remembers a war thinks to himself, *Really, we envy them. We'd love to be boys again, laughing our asses off, while old guys scream at us out their windows. Can't go back, though.*

A few doors down, the first man types out *thug* and *fuck* all night long.

Reading the posts, the one who remembers a war thinks to himself, *All you can do if you're old and angry is crown yourself King of the Witches, damn all the kids to hell, go to bed and, tomorrow, wake up in a mood.*

Dell Av

Dell is an avenue, its bridges arcing over small fish too quick in the water to name. Along the footpaths, out-of-town guests walk behind their hosts. On either side, front doors open into living rooms and kitchens where realtors offer tours. This is how we learn what living here is like.

Mallards float southwest on Howland Canal and northeast on Carroll, dive for small crustaceans, surface and dive again. Before we enter the empty house, we watch a while. Afterwards, we watch again.

If we lived here, we'd watch the birds day after day.

We return home wishing we were born into that other life, that rarer life, that life as iridescent as the mallard's green cheek.

Boone Av

Born a small footpath, Boone Avenue came of age in thick-settled North Carolina. Boone Avenue wasn't happy in those parts. Boone Avenue wanted room to wander.

So Boone Avenue walked out on North Carolina. *Too settled,* Boone Avenue said. Boone Avenue led wagon and wife to liberty, like Joseph led Mary to Egypt with baby Jesus. Boone Avenue said to his wife, *Kentucky's our Egypt.*

But civilization came for them, and that old dissatisfaction darkened their Kentucky farm. So Boone Avenue told the wife, *Indiana's our Egypt.* But civilization wasn't put off. Found them there, too.

Said Boone Avenue, *Missouri's our Egypt. Has to be.* But around midnight, civilization crept up to Missouri, hemming it in. Boone Avenue, ever the slick street, skedaddled.

From one west to the next, Boone Avenue moved on, two steps ahead of politicos, speculators, and side streets that sidled too close to Boone Avenue's business.

Boone Avenue wested all the way to California. Near the beach, Boone Avenue built a cabin of eucalypt wood thatched with palm fronds. Boone Avenue, by this time an old rutted street, figured he was finally free.

It didn't take long for bulldozers to knock at Boone Avenue's door. The dozers said, *Sir, this land is zoned R-1. No hunting. No outhouses or haylofts. Here's the Building Code. See for yourself.*

Again, Boone Avenue looked west. But Boone Avenue had run out of west. Out west was nothing but salt water. Boone Avenue's fugitive days were done.

Next morning, Boone Avenue heard the bulldozers roughing it towards him. Boone Avenue had never loved cities. Now, he was surrounded. He took out his rifle and pointed it straight up, right into his jaw's soft underside. Boone Avenue shot himself dead.

The dozers flayed Boone Avenue's body, tanned the stretched skin, and divided the hide into house lots.

Out of respect, they kept the name.

Westering out cross-continentally, Boone was an American street. Some die so that others might live free in three thousand square feet, four en suite, and Corian counters.

Pioneers! O Pioneers!

Thatcher Yard

encampment on Thatcher Yard—homeless
with their shit—pools of garbage—reported
this to police—they—our neighborhood
once a fine neighborhood

—from conversations among neighbors, Nextdoor.com

At Thatcher Yard, the City once repaired equipment, this when
Venice Beach, that pump-jacked oil-slicked redlined Slum-by-the-Sea,
lived out its lives in low-rise bungalows, flats, and squats for rent
to hairdressers, bricklayers, pensioned widows, teachers, drifters,
mechanics, and janitors. Painters painted pictures. Poets

wrote all night and burned their manuscripts at dawn because for fuck's
sake if you want the glory, fucking write for television.
January tides stormed cold with expatriate syllables.
Named for Venice, Italy, this place was like that other one
before its tourist century—home to butchers, charwomen,

and near-aristos who turned palazzi into pensioni.
Barely keeping house above the tide, they let to retired
politicos and disgraced literati whose subalterns
took the dankest rooms. A loveliness like that is hard to love,
but Henry James, he dressed that City up in perfumed yardage

to resist the stagnant summer reek of shit and rotting fish.
Venice was an open sewer then but James's readers walked
above all that. Bound in blue cloth, gilt-lettered, collectible
—volumes beautiful as any city. To read the book,
the buyer slit apart the uncut pages with a pen knife,

sniffed the deckled edges and inhaled fragrant washed-white paper.
No hint of sewer in it. So I understand my neighbors'
disillusion. I too have heard the man at Rose and Lincoln
scream and scream and I was robbed and I've seen needles, condoms
and the sidewalk's puddled piss, but things are complicated and

ghetto is a Venice word: *Ghetto Nuovo* where smelters
slagged their slop and La Serenissima Repubblica di
Venezia dumped its filthy Jews my kin and locked us up
within the walls at sundown. Neighbors say they want those people
out of here. *We don't mean harm, but what about our children and*

the ugliness? When speaking confidentially, my neighbors
say they'd like to truck that human garbage to a desert town,
turn them out in Barstow, build a tented camp in Victorville.
Make them fucking work! What my neighbors really want is camp guards
booted black and badged, Academy-equipped to disinfect

the streets. The young cadets are taught *they really must police* some-
times (not the job the trainees want but, yes, the job my neighbors
hire them to do). My neighbors want a beachside Henry James:
cleaned-up streets for people who will pay the bed and breakfast rent,
walk the Sunday boardwalk, burn their beach skins on the lemon sand

(for the problem children, belligerent or sad, there's a well-
reputed sanatorium up north in Canyon Country).
Throughout the Middle Sea, Venetian arms kept a kind of peace
and what my neighbors really want is a stiletto from the
Serenissima. Melt a pig of iron. Hammer hot

and fold it. Hammer hot and fold it. Hammer hot and hone that
edge to cut the uncut pages of an antiquary's book.
The slag—the lime, the lead, the sulfur—truck it to the ghetto
with its dirty people who refuse to pay the market rate.
Now, open the book. Its laundered pages freshen indoor air.

Lucille Av

A virtuous street, lawns clipped and tidy, its signage a caution to neighbors. No graffiti slurs masonry. No body sleeps on pavement. House lots are small. Mortgages conform. Cars park legally.

At one end of the street, an all-way stop slows traffic to a residential pace. At the other end, a church.

Outsiders, here for boardwalk and beach, don't bother with Lucille, never walk that mile east.

Lucille won't walk west to meet them. The avenue stays put, hoarding neighbors behind hedges. Though they're on the map, some streets do not exist for strangers.

Westminster Dog Park

No dogs in the dog park today—

but on Westminster Avenue

a dog, alone,

trots toward the beach.

IV

» Washington Bl «

At the Union Pacific sidings, each yellow diesel shows off its American flag. Each diesel is numbered: 5033, 4903, 4168. Taggers add white cab-tall call letters: *NEMsJOES. NRA. HERES. OTIS KINKR.*

Before Christmas, Dad would drive us out to these railyards where roustabouts tossed Christmas trees down from the boxcars. The Christmas Tree Man nailed each tree to a rough-hewn cruciform stand.

We weren't Christians. We weren't Jews. We believed in nothing. But we'd buy a tree and cinch its hulk to the Dodge Dart's roof. We'd bring it home, stand it tall in the picture window, and decorate it with angel hair and tinsel. Pine resin stuck to my fingertips, cleaned with a stiff scrub brush and borax that abraded the skin. Resin dripped down my shirtfront, stained the living room carpet. Those stains never came out.

Loading the tree, Dad would look out at the boxcars. *Did I ever tell you about Uncle Charlie? Faked his age, joined the Navy, sailed with Theodore Roosevelt's Great White Fleet, lived not far from here. Before you were born, he took a train to see the family in Chicago. Never showed up. Days later they found him, bruised and concussed, wandering the Omaha railyards. The railroad company shipped his body back to L.A.*

The otherselves have heard this story before. While we drive by, they scan the railyard. Uncle Charlie and *OTIS KINKR*—they're out there somewhere, stumbling among the flatbed trailers stacked three high. They're confused and hungry. They're looking for signs. Uncle Charlie has a suitcase. Otis Kinkr's brought a spray can. There are signs, alright: *AT & SF Railway Property / NO TRESPASSING / OR LOITERING / NO PARKING / SEMI-TRAILERS UNATTACHED WILL BE TOWED AWAY.* It's too late. Charlie is dead. Otis is missing.

Still, the signs direct mind towards memory. What those signs say is true, all of it. Unattached semi-trailers, illegally parked, *are* towed. Trespassers *do* loiter. OTIS KINKR *was* here. Uncle Charlie *is* missing, Dad *is* dead.

Behind me, downtown flashes its phosphors. Window glass fragments the sunlight.

Santa Clara Av

On this block five years back, Oscar D— takes a bullet, bleeds out and dies. He has *no known gang affiliations.* The County Coroner holds Oscar D—'s body for further examination. Winter rains wash the splatter into the culverts.

Santa Clara Avenue knows nothing about it. Santa Clara is an object, a thing made of sand, gravel, and tar. It doesn't know the quake of its own traffic or the weight of its own dead. Santa Clara doesn't write sympathy cards.

Maybe, somewhere on earth, there's a city more fully alive to human feeling.

Not ours. Not yet.

Navarre Ct & Alhambra Ct

Navarre Court and Alhambra Court are alleys. Near their juncture, a utility pole. My city names every utility pole, that name stamped on an aluminum tag nailed into the wood. This is the name at Navarre and Alhambra:

3

6

6

6

7

1

M

44—8—157

44—8—38

44—8—158

XP 138—162

My city also names its manhole covers, sewer lines, gas meters, and cell towers.

Mine is an ordered city, self-aware and conscientious. My city catalogues streets, off-ramps, and taxable acreage. Mine is the numerate city, legible to all with eyes to see.

My city's cameras watch me as I walk.

Just now, my city's attention is elsewhere: on a burst water main, a downed power line, a jackknifed big rig. At XP 138—162, I am visible but unseen.

The Dead

In California's Venice, neighbors die daily. We die in our sleep or we die wide awake. We die numb or in agony, of old age or of knife wounds. We stroke out. Our hearts stop. We overdose. It's the liver. It's the colon. It's the lungs. It's everything at once.

Italy's Venice, my neighborhood's namesake, keeps its dead close by. From the water, the Cimitero di San Michele glows like sun-dried bone. Within, visitors tour tombs and monuments. In that Adriatic Venice, everyone remembers that men and women live and die.

My Venice, a burlesque of its Italian Other, dredges its own canals and preserves its own colonnades. But we refuse to live among the dead. We no more want to see an offshore island cemetery than we want an oil rig.

Should San Michele's illustrious ghosts decide to haunt our Venice rather than their own, we'll string our kayaks and canoes with holiday lights. Brodsky! Pound! Stravinsky! Diaghilev! For you, an ecstatic boat parade! Stay a night! Stay three! But, no, not eternity.

Anyway, we have heroes of our own to honor, neighbors who don't expect to die but die despite themselves. Dead bus drivers. Dead welders. Dead doctors and dead housekeepers. Dead dressmakers, painters, teachers, and engineers. Dead women, men, and stillborn infants.

Discreetly, their bodies vanish from our streets.

In this entire beach town, we reserve just one room for our deceased: VIP Mortuary offers *the finest service in individual pet cremation.*

Eastern Ct

Read the signs.

Don't park between ten and twelve. Put out your trash on Tuesdays.

And stop looking. There is no Western Court.

Who are you, that you don't know this?

Clune Av

At 10 p.m., Ms. P— steps out of her car. A man comes out of nowhere, screaming obscenities.

He towers over her. He rages. *You'd best be dead,* he hollers.

She stands as still as a utility pole.

He looms and shouts, but he doesn't touch her. His fingertips never lose control or fold into a fist. His feet, like hers, are fixed to the pavement.

A neighbor calls police. The obscene man hears the siren. Finally, he steps back and runs, eluding the foot pursuit and the helicopter spotlight.

An officer takes a report from the woman, whose voice and hands shake as she speaks. She vomits on the officer's shoes. *I'm sorry,* she says to the uniform. *Sorry.*

The neighbors, clustered a little way off, talk quietly among themselves. Some have had run-ins with the night man. Everyone knows him. He has a blanket around his shoulders or he's in a hoodie. It's gray, it's blue. He wears a patchy beard. He's clean-shaven. His front teeth are yellow—no, they're missing. He smells. He's thirty. He's fifty. He's White. He's Mexican.

Everyone knows that he's crazy. An alcoholic. On fentanyl. Sleeps in his car. Sleeps on the beach. Has a tent on 3rd Street. Look at the way he stood over that woman, straight back, shoulders squared up. For sure he's a vet.

Does anyone know the woman? Does she live around here?

One neighbor, a retired prosecutor, says the man made a *criminal threat,* as defined by California Penal Code section 422(a). A woman—another attorney?—says it's way more than a threat. Ms. P— feared for her life. She's thinking Penal Code section 240, *assault.*

Truth is beauty. The neighbors are regal tonight in their truth. Under the streetlight, clothed in their knowing, the neighbors, resplendent, shimmer.

Meanwhile, the vanishing night man runs as fast as he can in every direction.

Meanwhile, doubled over and retching, Ms. P— says, *Sorry. I'm so sorry.*

Later, neighbors walk back to their homes. Later, their bedrooms dark, they speak softly to significant others.

Yeah, they say, *We saw the guy. We saw the woman. We called police.*

Listen for footsteps in case he comes back.

Listen for hooves, for unclipped claws clacking on concrete.

Let me tell you.

Let me tell you.

Rennie Av

In ninety years, the house on Rennie has had ten owners.

These ten called themselves *I* and called this house *mine*.

In 1973, one *I*, on her last day in this house, remembered the terra-cotta floor, cool on the soles of her feet. In 1948, another *I*, his boxes stacked in the hallway, already missed the two swans frosted into the shower door's glass. In 1937, the first *I*, living in her daughter's back room, dreamed about vodka and tonic, the lemon tree's fruit, and the patio, serene in July.

Today, in a hospice bed, morphine managing pain, the tenth *I* remembers casement windows and red roof tile. The bed, on the first floor, has a view of the garden.

This tenth *I* and every *I* before him have claimed the grace of an arched entry, vermillion fuchsias on either side, moisture condensed on their petals. Every *I* has declared the dwarf roses *mine* and has claimed both the guavas and the geraniums.

Of the ten, one planted bougainvillea against the side of the house. Another installed carpet in the bedroom. A third tore the carpet up: *Who would hide such a beautiful hardwood floor?* One hooked up all-electric appliances; another, all-gas. So distinct in their desires.

After the tenth, others will come. Perhaps a couple: one, a school teacher; the other, a quality control engineer. Or: one, an emergency dispatcher; the other, an actor. Or: one, an insurance broker; the other, a supermarket manager.

Once they're settled in, they may set up a telescope, angling it toward the moon. They may hang an iron skillet from a kitchen hook or replace the backyard charcoal grill with propane.

One day, this couple's children, now adults, will take their aging parents aside. *You've been falling a lot. Don't you think it's time to sell? What if you fall on the stairs? Then what?*

The children are right. Then what.

Ironsides St

Ironsides Street is a walk street. Not a car drives by. Not many neighbors watch from their windows.

Here you can jimmy a lock, take what's worth taking, and get yourself out. Ten minutes tops.

A couple returns to their burglarized home.

> *We have an alarm,* he tells her. *This place should have been safe.*

> *Of course it's not safe,* she says. *It has a door, doesn't it?*

Marine Ct

A red light on Marine. No break in traffic.

Beyond the light are beachside parking lots and bike paths. Beyond these, tractor-groomed sand. Then water, turquoise out to the white horizon.

What's beyond that edge? The Pillars of Hercules. The Garden of the Hesperides. The Slumbering Sun's Summer Palace.

There's not a wife in Venice who paces a widow-walk, straining her eyes towards a mainmast's return. Not one neighbor in a hundred knows a fishery from a bathtub.

We live in a beach town. Ocean is a foreign country. Driving west, we stop the car well short of drowning.

Coeur D'Alene Av

Overhead, green canopy and shaded arcade, the work of tipu trees.

The trees seem tame. Don't kid yourself: They're unteachable beasts.

Beneath the roadbed, roots as round as human thighs knit thickets curb to curb, shallow and deep in the beachtown alluvium. Roots lift sidewalk slabs. Roots shatter curbs, heaving cement shards up and out. This is a *root encroached* avenue.

The city surveils these tipus. The municipal code authorizes the Bureau of Street Services to clear-cut an avenue's shade if it gets out of hand.

Though wild and willful, the tipu is a patient tree. Months before Man's Last Day on Earth, the Bureau's staff will abandon their work. They'll huddle at home with their families, awaiting the apocalyptic end.

On that day, the tipus of Coeur D'Alene will free themselves of every concrete encumbrance. They'll break into classrooms and homes. They'll march across Venice, an army of trunk and bough.

Hear me, O Venice: Arbor Day is coming.

What Will You Do Without Us, Streets?

What will you do without us, streets, on the morning we neighbors pack our possessions and flee, the Pacific back-slapping our shadows as we stumble east?

What will you do when we give up your sea-slick sidewalks and slippery asphalt?

Our house numbers will vanish, our property lines buried in silt and raw salt.

To remain with you, we'd have to slit our own throats and fish out our unused gills. Our fingers would melt into fins. Our legs would fuse into flukes.

That life without a hand or foot: It's not for us.

As we leave you, we'll shred mortgages and rental agreements. No sense in these heirlooms. Once we go, we're gone. We won't tell the grandchildren we lived along-side you. What is there to say? We were here and then we weren't. That's no story they need to know.

Goodbye, streets. Like sideways sand crabs, we have a tidal surge to outrun. When we return, we will speak another language. Don't expect us to remember you. We will forget it all. You'll forget, too. You'll drown, and then you'll forget.

Venice Pier

Right off the pier, there's halibut, kelp bass, jacksmelt, surfperch, and mackerel.

No limits, no license. Line, reel, and knife are all you need.

Bloodworm will catch you most anything. For jacksmelt, try soft-shelled sand crab.

Start at sunrise. Set yourself up. Stay all day. Nobody hassles you.

If it's been raining, don't eat what you catch. What's flushed from the storm drains gets into the flesh. Heavy metals and pesticides. Sewage.

Best days to fish: hot days, three years into drought, ash blowing down from the canyons. Those days, you have the place to yourself. You won't believe the sunsets. Hard to breathe, but plenty of fish.

Flower Av

At the corner of Flower and Lincoln, a single-story structure, fifteen thousand square feet, zoned for commercial development.

This property has witnessed all five Ages of Man.

First the Age of Used Books. Decades ago, a bookstore was here, a firetrap of a business, back issues of *Playboy* and *Sunset* in boxes, the boxes in stacks, the stacks leaning against rough bookcases roughly nailed from pine slats. Silverfish gnawed at the mildewed pages. On floors and shelves, rat droppings. Above, long fluorescent tubes whose timid wattage failed to rout the shadows and their odors. After some years, this bookstore closed. A sign, *For Lease,* appeared.

Then the Age of Furniture Stores. At first, new neighbors wanted Indonesian nightstands sculpted from teak. Then Moroccan-tiled patio tables. Then sea green storage units hauled from Eastern Europe's post-Communist flotsam. Then custom-made sofas and loveseats. Then life-size Buddhas (seated) and beatific St. Francises (standing).

Then the Age of Antiques on Consignment: gilt imitations of French imitations of Roman and Greek originals. White marble, white gold, onyx jewelry, halogen-lit, each item a precious gift.

Then, for long years, no tenant at all. Windows broken and boarded, a place for people without place. Some lived in cars piled with scavenged possessions. Some lived on sidewalks, backs against retaining walls, exhausted and gaunt. No one had greater need for Siddhartha and St. Francis, but the holy men left the building long before.

Then a sign appeared, black and orange, twenty feet long: *Halloween SuperStore! Costumes—Masks—Makeup. HUGE! Open Late!* And so began the Age of Halloween, the Age of Haunting Children. It lasted forty days and nights before giving up the ghost.

And now the signs announce the Age of Demolition. Crews will salvage what they can. The rest will go to landfill.

We are a fallen people. We still have far to fall.

V
» Washington Bl «

The Rio Hondo channel is a concrete culvert, two walls and a damp floor. I remember my mother's rememberings, spoken aloud: How, in the last century's hundred Januaries, *it rains for days at a time.* How *the runoff scours the city's slopes and the city floods so bad you can't step off a curb without getting soaked to mid-calf.* How *neighbors park their cars at the curb, doors unlocked. What you'd do is walk to a stranger's car, open the passenger-side door, close it behind you, slide your butt across the bench seat, open the driver's side door, and set your boots on the street's unflooded crown.*

The otherselves point to my right, just beyond Rosemead. At the bridge over the Rio Hondo, a man in black T-shirt and shin-torn 501s pushes a shopping cart piled with fabric bags, each bag fat with fabric.

I have cousins. Cousins I've never met. Cousins who've disappeared. Cousins who've died. Cousins who walked off the face of the earth. Cousins not even Aunt Nettie could find. Cousin O— out on a street in some Pacific Coast city, donating plasma for thirty bucks a pint. That could be O— right there. Never met him. He could look like anyone.

The otherselves tell me they've seen this before. I remember their remembering. I'm their ghost.

Instant City

Once ours was mudflat and scrubland,
breezes quieter than voices,
quieter than moles or egrets
or the cougar-haunted mule deer.

Light and stillness—
creature-plash among the green-gray
acres, the slow oar's slow water
in the further gray, an ocean.

Then bulldozed landfill, sewer lines,
fiber cables, poured foundation,
steel beam supports, wood framing,
finished toilets, bedrooms, kitchens—

this Instant City, purpose-built
Contraption-on-Alluvium,
our California Chandigarh,
Brasilia, Vegas, Milton Keynes.

You and I are sudden people,
arrivistes from other somewheres
in this, our beach town, cold with June
mortgages and rents due on the first.

Brooks Av

On the security feed, four soundless stained glass windows at shoulder height, small and square, shatter. A white kid, hands in pockets, walks out of camera range like nothing's happened.

A hate crime, says the Pastor.

The Police Department's Watch Commander will not jump to that conclusion. *There's broken glass, sure, and a rock, and the hand that threw it, and the young man in the video. And we know that Bethel is predominantly Black. But,* he tells the Pastor, *we can't say more than that. Criminal intent is like the soul itself. It's not exactly writ upon the skin.*

The Watch Commander knows his Baptist teachings. A body may appear to tremble, as if in terror of the Lord. Yet deep within, undisclosed to others, the heart itself is obdurate and cold. Only Jesus knows the why of what we do.

The Watch Commander tells the Pastor, *Once we find him, rest assured, we'll question that young man. With luck and skill, we'll find the fat malignancy of motive feeding on that poor boy's rage. He could just be crazy, hearing voices telling him to break things.*

The Pastor shakes his head. The police—they think it's all about the windows.

He tells the Watch Commander, *Motive goes back further than you'd like to think. It's broken glass begat by brick, begat by hard-swung arm, begat by history, begat by sin, a chain of custody writ deep—older than the boy, the window, or the street-lit city. Sometimes, Lieutenant, a thing's exactly what it seems.*

Courtland St

In every season, lesions open on Courtland Street. In a city of sixty thousand streets, many are worse. Maintenance crews are small. Courtland waits its turn.

It's a long wait. Year by year, malignancies pock the pavement. Streetflesh oozes from open wounds. Asphalt scree scabs the gutter.

One morning, the Bureau of Street Services (Resurfacing and Reconstruction Division) closes the street to through traffic. They start work. Into each abscess, a rubber hose extrudes thick black unguent. In an eighth-inch layer over the grafted skin, the crew sprays a slurry sealant consisting of water, asphalt emulsion, aggregate, and additives. Then they pack their gear and move on.

Now Courtland's surface is smooth to the touch. We drive with delight, afloat on the placid roadbed.

Two streets away, another block blisters. A wound gapes, and winter rain, like a reptile's toxic saliva, dissolves the interior tissues. The front passenger tire hammers into the pit. No city is ever wholly saved.

Linnie Canal

It is early, overcast and cold. Near the canal's embankment, the children's park is empty. Beneath two swings, a yellow plastic slide, and a fairy-tale bridge, there's a carpet of beach sand.

Affixed to a gate is a sign: *Dogs must be kept on leash*. Another sign says, *No dogs allowed*.

The park prohibits all of the following: bikes, skateboards, roller skates, scooters, litter, and alcohol. Persons using this park will not feed the ducks, abandon animals, or endanger wildlife.

Beyond the signage, a gull, its gray wings fully spread, pecks at a doll's discarded arm.

The gull looks towards me. I return its gaze.

We two are radically estranged, each unable to imagine what it is to be the other. Still, for a long moment, we watch one another. I see no sign of recognition.

Now the slow wings move, and the gull, an airship, heaves itself above the jungle gym, hovers, and floats west, over the Pacific.

I stay behind with the doll's arm, the child's garden, and the written rules. Without wings, I can't get much further.

Ozone Av

A neighbor on Ozone Avenue asks me, *Why write about streets? Why not write about people? It's like your streets are empty.*

My neighbor is right. I sweep my streets clean of crowds. I lock neighbors in their rooms. Not one of these stick figures has a name. Some I call *you*. Some I call *we*. Most I call *neighbor*.

A woman I knew in college smoked clove cigarettes and opened her dorm room to parties. Bowie orbited her turntable.

I couldn't hear myself think. I sat on the carpet, back to the wall. I stared at her windows, her electrical outlets, the smoke from her ashtrays. Week after week, lost in white noise.

Nothing has changed. I like the lonesome last dark, just before sunrise. I like empty afternoon sidewalks and dark rooms, pensive at night.

I explain to my neighbor, *These poems, they're a little like still lifes.*

My name isn't neighbor, she says.

Pier Av

A man walks into Rocco's bookstore.

He says to Rocco, apropos of nothing,
I lived here. In Venice Beach. Forty years ago.

From behind the counter, Rocco says,
It's changed a lot since then.

The man says,
I lived on the Canals.
The house isn't there anymore.

Yeah, says Rocco.
Can't go home again.

The man pauses, his eyes
on a rack of paperbacks.

I'm in San Leandro now, he says.

So that's home, says Rocco.

No, says the man.
Not really.

Berkeley Dr

A cypress grows behind a front yard fence. Behind that tree, a house: a single floor, a stucco cube. The shades are drawn, the walls are gray. Magazines peek out from the mailbox. The sun warms Berkeley Drive. It's 4 p.m. Nothing is at risk.

Of a childhood friend, Czesław Miłosz wrote, *He sought strong flavors. He fled from kitsch.* Berkeley Drive is far from Poland and very far from 1940. Still, Miłosz's wartime friend can't have been the last such man. Why not another? Why not right here, on this block?

Scan the street. Look out for someone drawn to resinous scents. Look for a serious face—serious, but skeptical.

Yours, for instance. Don't you seek strong flavors? Don't you shrink from sentiment? Aren't you convinced of the past and its power? Don't you sometimes wonder whether neighbors fly toward history's klieg-lit heat like moths towards nightmare?

To be honest, I don't know if that tree really is a cypress.

But the tree doesn't care. Like other living things, it answers to any name we give it. It shares its fragrance without asking. There, at least, is a saving grace.

Venice Bl

In adjacent second story apartments live an old she and an old he.

She is disabled, living in her unit thanks to Section 8.

He is retired.

There's no AC—who needs it so close to the beach?—so they sit in separate recliners in separate apartments, sweating and watching cable. She's in a muumuu. He's in boxers. Her chin sags. She looks like a chicken. His belly protrudes as if it's a tumor.

Both silently suffer their maladies. She takes prednisone, smears clobetasol on her elbows, and refrigerates her Humalog. He sits next to a metal tank wearing a tube that feeds oxygen into his nostrils. Once a day, he fits a face mask over his nose and mouth, inhaling Albuterol from a nebulizer. He used to sit next to the pool inhaling a joint. Not now. Smoking inside the apartment can get him evicted.

Both are close to death. It's not days away, not even weeks. But death will come fairly soon. No more than, say, a year. They've both stacked the shock of a doctor's *I'm sorry* with the other important papers. Both the old he and the old she are lucid. They just don't want to dwell.

Theirs is an endless exhaustion. Neither of them talks about it. Neither says *The pain is unbearable* or *I can't live like this anymore*. It is unbearable. They can't live like this anymore. But what can they do? When it gets bad, he takes Vicodin. She takes oxycodone. Some days, if the dosage is right, they almost forget.

They met when he moved in. In the three years since, they've hardly seen each other except once when, escorted by middle-aged sons, they returned to the complex at the same moment from separate outings. Their adult children eyed each other warily, ashamed at how little it matters no matter what you do.

He and she eyed each other warily too, ashamed of their children and ashamed of themselves.

Later, sitting alone in their own apartments, neither of them can figure it out. *Why should I feel ashamed?* they ask themselves. *I'm the one who's dying.*

Louella Av

Honeybees hover above lavender stalks. They are six-legged cats. They do not buzz. They purr. For long moments, they consider each flower in turn. Then they pounce.

I stand to the side. Neither flower nor bee knows that I am a creature. Neither knows that I watch. I am beyond their awareness, as is the street, as is the city.

A hummingbird perceives my slight movement and lightnings away.

Alone on Louella, that bird sees me for what I am.

Lizard

As I'm sitting with my coffee, an alligator lizard startles out from under a shrub, darts over my bare foot, and slides under a planting box.

I remember this creature's ancient kin running the hillpaths and housewalls. That was decades ago. These days, they're scarce. No skinks, no toads. No garter or king snakes. Backyard birdcalls go quiet after 10 a.m. Monarchs arrive in the backyard one at a time, settling for half a minute on the milkweed. They used to gather in fluttering clouds.

When I was ten, I captured as many small creatures as I could, holding them in Maxwell House coffee cans. I rubber-banded wax paper around the rim. I punched air holes with the point of a Bic.

I meant to keep them alive. Every one of them died in my care.

This lizard's too small to know that history. For the lizard, my foot is stone and I am wall.

Woodlawn Av

Confident on the scaffolding, two men shroud the exterior with Jumbo Tex Fortifiber. Winter storms are months away, but this job will take time. The scrap lumber heaps up like mining slag.

Elsewhere on the street, iris, lantana, and bougainvillea shroud fat clapboards. How long can these wooden houses last?

Smithson, his ghost at my side, whispers:

> *buildings don't*
> *fall into ruin*
> *after they are built*
>
> *but rather*
> *rise into ruin*
> *before they are built*
>
> *ruins in reverse*

Ghosts, too, are ruins-in-reverse, falling away from death's entropy towards articulate *spiritus*. Some ghosts prophesy, predicting the irrational past. Eyes see. Ears hear. Dead lumber assembles itself, becoming a house even the living can haunt.

Peacock

In the first month of the plague, the bird escapes a yard and all year long drags his dreamy gown along the streets.

The neighbors post photos. Here he is on Strongs. On Tivoli. At the Grand Canal. At Redwood Avenue, Northstar, Mast, Victoria, Marine, Dewey.

One neighbor writes to all the others, *Saw him crossing Venice Boulevard today. One car had to swerve. Came close to killing him. Someone up there must be watching over him.*

The neighbors name him and wonder if there are others. Someone says she's seen the hens. No noise complaints, though they scream like newborns, peacocks.

A friend says, *There was that film, forty or fifty years ago. Small town. First snow of the season. A fountain on the plaza, the water frozen while it fell. From nowhere, a peacock flies in—lands right next to the fountain. Fans his feathers like it's spring. In the movie, it means something.*

Later, online, someone says, *We need this beauty now.*

Someone else replies, *What beauty? He's a dirty bird. More crap to clean.*

Another: *He's beautiful, but he's not safe. There's psychos here who hacksaw bills off pelicans. Last week, someone drowned a clutch of ducklings at that park in Playa. People are insane, and no one gives a shit.*

Another: *Wild dogs could kill him just as easy. Doesn't take a lunatic.*

Another: *The Council should just trap the bird. Palos Verdes traps its peacocks all the time and takes them to the Arboretum.* In the end, that's just what the Council does.

Later, when the plague years end, the homebound talk of watching from their windows. *It was magical,* a neighbor says. Iridescent green and midnight blue: We want our moment back.

Gardenias

Gardenias are old-neighbor flowers, blossoming in the last century. They ornament old homes, clapboard homes, the greened-up yards moistened by oscillating sprinklers.

So, too, the lantanas. One night in an ancient annum, when Venice, California, lawned from end to end, a Douglas Aircraft engineer said to his wife, *Let's plant lantanas. They'll bring butterflies.* And so, in that wide front yard, lantanas luminesced, bright as color TVs.

In that same annum, mothers warned their children, *Don't eat the oleander—it's poisonous.* Against dark green leaves, narrow as lancets, little white flowers glowed ice-white. No one thought to pull it out.

And in that annum, a schoolteacher, an East Coast transplant, asked her neighbor, *What's an avocado?* The neighbor taught her how to turn the fruit into a *festive Mexican dip,* gave her a few limes, and made her coffee.

That was the day the hollyhocks bloomed, some pink, some blue, wide as sun-faced stars. A visiting cousin said, *Hollyhocks need heat. Can't grow 'em at the beach.* But the hollyhocks had rooted deep, grown beanstalk-tall in empty lots and untended side yards.

In those days, swallowtails, bumblebees, and cabbage whites flocked like birds. Salamanders burrowed under garden border brickwork. Summer rains forced worms to surface. Beached on sidewalk concrete, there was no way back. Red ants fought centipedes for all that good jerked meat.

The salamanders are long gone. Haven't seen red ants in years. Weak with whiteflies and mildew, the old plantings wilt. Neighbors sleep on mattresses stuffed with bad news.

But look here: White and scarlet gardenias edge a yard round an old house on 6th and Brooks. A lemon tree fruits. A milkweed flowers. Miles into summer, so much lives on.

VI
» Washington Bl «

The intersection with Whittier: This is the end of Washington Boulevard.

We're tired of driving, me and my otherselves. At the end of the pilgrimed road, there's just another street. We could drive for days and never get anywhere else. We make a U and head on back.

Venice knows nothing about Ed's Distribution, nothing of Rude Boys, nothing of convoyed cement mixers, beam bridges or Pratt trusses. Facing the beach, Venice zones against transmission ball bearings, the Union Pacific, and the Rio Hondo.

But my phone rings in Venice. My mailbox is full. I have appointments and neighbors. There's an ocean, the Pacific. I live at its edge, my otherselves behind me.

Notes

The two-letter street abbreviations—Av, Bl, Dr, Ct, and so on—follow conventions of Los Angeles Bureau of Street Services signage.

In "Preston Wy," "we confuse numbness for well-being" is taken from Jen Hofer's poem "Dear Data" in *Conditions/Conditioning*, a chapbook co-written with TC Tolbert. Though I attribute the remark to an "out-of-town guest," the San Francisco-born Hofer resides in L.A.

The machine sent toward the star Aldebaran in "Aldebaran Canal" is Pioneer 10, launched in 1972. On its current trajectory, Pioneer 10 will reach the vicinity of Aldebaran in about two million years.

The term "surfurbia," in "L.A. Louver Gallery," comes from Reyner Banham's indispensable *Los Angeles: An Architecture in Four Ecologies* (Harper & Row, 1971). David Hockney lived in the Hollywood Hills until 2019, just after this piece was written.

"Venice Marine Biological Station" quotes the United States National Museum, Smithsonian Institution, *Report on the Progress and Condition of the United States National Museum for the Year Ending June 30, 1921*.

In "Berkeley Dr," "*He sought strong flavors...*" is taken from Czesław Miłosz, *Miłosz's ABCs* (Farrar Straus & Giroux, 2001). In its original setting, the sentence describes Dostoevsky, whose novels Miłosz taught and admired but whose underlying philosophy he distrusted. The sentence reminds me strongly of Miłosz's assessments, in *The Captive Mind* and elsewhere, of certain friends in interwar and wartime Poland —so much so that, in the poem "Berkeley Dr," this is what it has become.

In "Venice Bl," Section 8 refers to a provision of the Housing Act of 1937 that provides supplementary rental vouchers to eligible tenants.

Smithson's lines in "Woodlawn Av" are taken from Robert Smithson, "A Tour of the Monuments of Passaic, New Jersey," *Artforum*, December 1967.

"Peacock" references Federico Fellini's *Amarcord* (1973).

Acknowledgments

Thanks to the following for publishing these poems, some in earlier form:

Aji Magazine: "Marine Court," "Peacock"
Altadena Literary Review: "Berkeley Dr," "Dell Av"
Ambit: "L.A. Louver Gallery"
Blue Unicorn: "At the Whole Foods Market"
Disquieting Muses Quarterly: "Santa Catalina Island Viewed from Venice Beach"
High Window: "Dimmick Av," "Coeur D'Alene Av"
Koan Kinship: "Vernon Av," "Venice Marine Biological Station," "What Will You Do
    Without Us, Streets?"
La Piccioletta Barca: "Venice Bl"
Lummox: "Lucille Av," "Mishkon & St. Mark's"
Masque & Spectacle: "Park Row"
Monday Night: "Ozone Av," "Preston Wy"
Moon & Sun Review: "The Dead," "Flower Av"
Oddville Press: "Rose Av"
PROEM: "Louella Av"
Rappahannock Review: "Navarre Ct & Alhambra Ct," "Santa Clara Av"
The Rupture: "26th Pl"
Slush Pile: "Gardenias"
Softblow: "Animalia," "Union Jack St," "Courtland St," "Horizon Av"
Spillway: "Pacific Division"
Stand Magazine: "Strongs Dr," "Venezia Av"
Words & Whispers: "Electric Av"

I am grateful to the creative communities that have welcomed me in and thought-fully responded to my work. I owe particular thanks to Laurel Ann Bogen and her Sunday morning circle: Fernando Castro, Marie Chambers, Elaina Eller, Shelley Holder, Jeff Rochlin, Amanda Scharf, and Jim Zukin. Thanks as well to Beyond Baroque's Wednesday night regulars: China Adams, Natalie Bowers, Ranney Campbell, Lynda Crawford, Gary Denk, Florence Elon, Alex Frankel, Lisa Giaffo, liz gonzalez, Peter Gordon, Elyse Hart, Doug Jacobs, James Evart Jones, Joel Katz, Shahé Mankerian, Ted Mico, Steve Miller, Tatiana Sulovska, and Constant Williams. For their support and encouragement, my gratitude to Beyond Baroque's Emmitt Conklin, Richard Modiano, Quentin Ring, and Jimmy Vega.

I owe deep gratitude to friends and family who devoted considerable time and attention to earlier drafts: Chris Ferris, Deirdre Gainor, Colleen Jaurretche, Ariel Laichas-Malamud, Donna Malamud, Beth Ruscio, Mike Shaler, Mike Sonksen, Susan Suntree, and Zoey Zimmerman. I am also especially fortunate to have found, in Diane Kistner of FutureCycle Press, a particularly thoughtful and meticulous editor. I am grateful for her sustained attention to this project.

Finally, I owe much to Bill Mohr, whose Beyond Baroque workshops on the history of L.A. poetics inspired this work. His book *Hold-Outs: The Los Angeles Poetry Renaissance, 1948-1992* is the place to start for anyone new to the territory.

My love always to Donna and Ari.

About FutureCycle Press

FutureCycle Press is dedicated to publishing lasting English-language poetry in both print-on-demand and Kindle formats. Founded in 2007 by long-time independent editor/publishers and partners Diane Kistner and Robert S. King, the press was incorporated as a nonprofit in 2012. A number of our editors are distinguished poets and writers in their own right, and we have been actively involved in the small press movement going back to the early seventies.

Each year, we award the FutureCycle Poetry Book Prize and honorarium for the best original full-length volume of poetry we published that year. Introduced in 2013, proceeds from our Good Works projects are donated to charity. Our Selected Poems series highlights contemporary poets with a substantial body of work to their credit; with this series we strive to resurrect work that has had limited distribution and is now out of print.

We are dedicated to giving all of the authors we publish the care their work deserves, offering a catalog of the most diverse and distinguished work possible, and paying forward any earnings to fund more great books. All of our books are kept "alive" and available unless and until an author requests a title be taken out of print.

We've learned a few things about independent publishing over the years. We've also evolved a unique and resilient publishing model that allows us to focus mainly on vetting and preserving for posterity poetry collections of exceptional quality without becoming overwhelmed with bookkeeping and mailing, fundraising activities, or taxing editorial and production "bubbles." To find out more about what we are doing, come see us at futurecycle.org.

The FutureCycle Poetry Book Prize

All original, full-length poetry books published by FutureCycle Press in a given calendar year are considered for the annual FutureCycle Poetry Book Prize. This allows us to consider each submission on its own merits, outside of the context of a traditional contest. Too, the judges see the finished book, which will have benefitted from the beautiful book design and strong editorial gloss we are famous for.

The book ranked the best in judging is announced as the prize-winner in January of the subsequent year. There is no fixed monetary award; instead, the winning poet receives an honorarium of 20% of the total net royalties from all poetry books and chapbooks the press sold online in the year the winning book was published. The winner is also accorded the honor of being on the panel of judges for the next year's competition; all judges receive copies of the contending books to keep for their personal library.